A LIFEGUIDE  BIBLE STUDY

JAMES

Faith That Works

11 Studies
for individuals or groups

Andrew T. & Phyllis J. Le Peau

With Notes for Leaders

INTERVARSITY PRESS
DOWNERS GROVE, ILLINOIS 60515

InterVarsity Press® is the book-publishing division of InterVarsity Christian Fellowship®, a student movement active on campus at hundreds of universities, colleges and schools of nursing in the United States of America, and a member movement of the International Fellowship of Evangelical Students. For information about local and regional activities, write Public Relations Dept., InterVarsity Christian Fellowship, 6400 Schroeder Rd., P.O. Box 7895, Madison, WI 53707-7895.

LifeGuide® is a registered trademark of InterVarsity Christian Fellowship.

Cover photograph: Robert McKendrick

ISBN 0-8308-1018-8

Printed in the United States of America ∞

31	30	29	28	27	26	25	24	23	22	21	20	19	18	17
10	09	08	07	06	05	04	03	02	01	00	99	98		

Contents

Getting the Most from LifeGuide Bible Studies   5

Introducing James   9

1   **James 1—5**   Faith That Works: James Overview   12

2   **James 1:1-18**   Dependable or Double-minded?   15

3   **James 1:19-27**   Words, Words, Words   18

4   **James 2:1-13**   Who's the Judge?   21

5   **James 2:14-26**   Just Works   24

6   **James 3:1-12**   On Preventing Forest Fires   27

7   **James 3:13—4:10**   Makers and Breakers of Peace   30

8   **James 4:11-17**   Getting Perspective   33

9   **James 5:1-11**   What Awaits   36

10   **James 5:12-20**   Making Others Whole   39

11   **James 1—5**   Faith That Works: James Review   42

Leader's Notes   45

Getting the Most
from LifeGuide Bible Studies

Many of us long to fill our minds and our lives with Scripture. We desire to be transformed by its message. LifeGuide Bible Studies are designed to be an exciting and challenging way to do just that. They help us to be guided by God's Word in every area of life.

How They Work

LifeGuides have a number of distinctive features. Perhaps the most important is that they are *inductive* rather than *deductive*. In other words, they lead us to *discover* what the Bible says rather than simply *telling* us what it says.

They are also thought provoking. They help us to think about the meaning of the passage so that we can truly understand what the author is saying. The questions require more than one-word answers.

The studies are personal. Questions expose us to the promises, assurances, exhortations and challenges of God's Word. They are designed to allow the Scriptures to renew our minds so that we can be transformed by the Spirit of God. This is the ultimate goal of all Bible study.

The studies are versatile. They are designed for student, neighborhood and church groups. They are also effective for individual study.

How They're Put Together

LifeGuides also have a distinctive format. Each study need take no more than forty-five minutes in a group setting or thirty minutes in personal study—unless you choose to take more time.

The studies can be used within a quarter system in a church and fit well in a semester or trimester system on a college campus. If a guide has more than thirteen studies, it is divided into two or occasionally three parts of approximately twelve studies each.

LifeGuides use a workbook format. Space is provided for writing answers to each question. This is ideal for personal study and allows group members to prepare in advance for the discussion.

The studies also contain leader's notes. They show how to lead a group discussion, provide additional background information on certain questions, give helpful tips on group dynamics and suggest ways to deal with problems which may arise during the discussion. With such helps, someone with little or no experience can lead an effective study.

Suggestions for Individual Study

1. As you begin each study, pray that God will help you to understand and apply the passage to your life.

2. Read and reread the assigned Bible passage to familiarize yourself with what the author is saying. In the case of book studies, you may want to read through the entire book prior to the first study. This will give you a helpful overview of its contents.

3. A good modern translation of the Bible, rather than the King James Version or a paraphrase, will give you the most help. The New International Version, the New American Standard Bible and the Revised Standard Version are all recommended. However, the questions in this guide are based on the New International Version.

4. Write your answers in the space provided in the study guide. This will help you to express your understanding of the passage clearly.

5. It might be good to have a Bible dictionary handy. Use it to look up any unfamiliar words, names or places.

Suggestions for Group Study

1. Come to the study prepared. Follow the suggestions for individual study mentioned above. You will find that careful preparation will greatly enrich your time spent in group discussion.

2. Be willing to participate in the discussion. The leader of your group will not be lecturing. Instead, he or she will be encouraging the members of the group to discuss what they have learned from the passage. The leader will be asking the questions that are found in this guide. Plan to share what God has taught you in your individual study.

3. Stick to the passage being studied. Your answers should be based on the verses which are the focus of the discussion and not on outside authorities such as commentaries or speakers. This guide deliberately avoids jumping from book to book or passage to passage. Each study focuses on only one passage. Book studies are generally designed to lead you through the book in the order in which it was written. This will help you follow the author's argument.

4. Be sensitive to the other members of the group. Listen attentively when they share what they have learned. You may be surprised by their insights! Link what you say to the comments of others so the group stays on the topic. Also, be affirming whenever you can. This will encourage some of the more hesitant members of the group to participate.

5. Be careful not to dominate the discussion. We are sometimes so eager to share what we have learned that we leave too little opportunity for others to respond. By all means participate! But allow others to also.

6. Expect God to teach you through the passage being discussed and through the other members of the group. Pray that you will have an enjoyable and profitable time together.

7. If you are the discussion leader, you will find additional suggestions and helpful ideas for each study in the leader's notes. These are found at the back of the guide.

Introducing James

Unlike most books of the New Testament, the letter of James is best known for the people who don't like it. It's seen as a scalawag among the obviously Christ-centered letters of Paul and the love-concerned writings of John. People like love. They like Christ. They don't like James.

James is harsh and dogmatic. We feel the sting of his words even today—"Don't be deceived," "You foolish man," "You adulterous people," "Now listen." We find James hard to take for good reason.

Of all the people who do not like James, Martin Luther is probably the most famous. Compared to the other solid New Testament writings, James, he felt, was full of straw—empty, hollow. He virtually relegated the letter to a position of lesser Scripture. He believed that it taught salvation by works. And that would never do for Martin "Salvation-by-Grace-Alone" Luther. Because of Luther's feelings and those of others like him, Protestant Christians have tended to ignore this book.

Yet the early church saw it as a book bearing apostolic authority and, more importantly, as a book that bore God's authority. James spoke a needed and empowered word to the churches. Thus it was included in the New Testament canon alongside Paul and John, carrying equal weight with their writings. Because it has been avoided and because it bears the full force of God's Word, James deserves our special study.

And what does it have to tell us? James is practical. Take problems. James knows nobody's life is perfect. So he doesn't tell us how to live trouble free, but how to live when troubles hit. Do we complain? Or do we use them as an opportunity for growth?

Take words. We all talk. And sometimes we say things we wish we hadn't. James helps us use words more carefully, more constructively. Do they hurt others? Do they advance God's kingdom? Are they truthful? Are they loving?

Take money. It flows around us (despite our protestations concerning tight budgets and taxes). Do we withhold it when others are in need? Do we put more value on worldly things than on the things of God?

Take time. If we have enough money, we know we never have enough time. We do all we can to get the most out of each hour of each day, filling our calendars with activity. But do we miss God's will and perspective in the midst of our schedule making?

James is practical—maybe too practical! So expect this study to be difficult—not because it will be hard to understand but because it will be all too easy to understand.

Who is this fellow James who makes us so uncomfortable? There are several people in the New Testament called James, including two apostles. Though they have never been completely certain, most church scholars have believed that a third man, James the brother of Jesus (Mt 13:55; Mk 6:3), wrote this letter. While he probably joined the others in Jesus' family in rejecting Jesus during his earthly ministry, James certainly started following Jesus after his resurrection. In fact, James soon became the head of the church in Jerusalem.

He probably led the first church council in Jerusalem (Acts 15), which decided that Gentiles did not have to become Jews before they could be saved. This is an important factor in assessing James's view of faith and works (which is to be noted in light of 2:14-26).

Yet James was aware of the very Jewish make-up of the church in Jerusalem and required Paul to squelch the rumor that he, Paul, was telling Jews to abandon the Law of Moses. James himself apparently followed Jewish law closely, enough so that he was known as James the Just. He died a martyr in A.D. 62.

James addresses his letter to "the twelve tribes scattered among the nations." The twelve tribes could refer to Jewish Christians which through exile, enslavement and trade were spread throughout the entire Mediterranean basin. More likely it refers simply to Christians since the New Testament compares the church to Israel (Gal 6:16 RSV; 1 Pet 2:9-10). In any case, the letter is not addressed to one specific congregation, as Paul's letters were. It is therefore called a general, or catholic, epistle.

The purpose of this guide is to help you face squarely James's call for a consistent Christian life, for a practical faith. We seek to do this through nine studies each covering about half a chapter. This may not seem like much, but James's proverblike compactness calls for it.

These nine studies are bracketed by two studies of the entire book. The first, an overview, helps you get a sweep of the book so you can put the middle nine studies in context. The second, a review, helps you put the nine back together, so you can go away with a cohesive view of James and a strong sense of how God wants you to grow.

You will not necessarily like James when you finish. But it is our prayer that through it God will give you a faith that works.

1
Faith That Works: James Overview

James 1—5

Most of the letters we get are warm, newsy notes. But every once in a while a letter comes along that is harder to read. It is full of love but also full of honest truth that may be difficult to take. We sense its rightness, but we also sense it could mean some painful changes for us.

In this first study we will look over the whole letter of James to get an overview of some basic issues we will explore more in later studies.

1. How do you respond when people say things to you that are hard to take?

2. Read James 1—5. What kind of person do you find James to be?

3. What do we know of the people James wrote his letter to?

4. Generally, what is the tone or atmosphere of the letter? (Harsh, kind, easygoing, loving, businesslike, something else?) Explain.

How do you respond to this tone?

5. What topics are discussed in the letter?

6. What kind of images and examples does James use?

7. What unifying theme, if any, do you see in the letter?

8. How is 1:26-27 expanded on in the rest of the letter?

9. What statements in the letter do you have the most difficulty with? Why?

10. What statements in the letter do you find most exciting and encouraging? Why?

11. Ask God to work in you through the study of James.

2
Dependable or Double-minded?

James 1:1-18

No pain. No gain. Or so the saying goes. Athletes remind themselves of this to get their best possible performance. Sometimes they have to go through grueling training. Without it, there is no improvement. James suggests it is the same for Christians.

1. "Getting in shape is simple. Just eat right and exercise regularly." Why do you find this easier said than done?

2. Read James 1:1-18. Why does it seem strange that we should "consider it pure *joy*" whenever we "face trials of many kinds" (v. 2)?

3. How are perseverance and maturity developed in us by enduring trials (vv. 3-4)?

4. What difficult experiences have increased your perseverance and maturity?

5. How might trials expose our need for God's wisdom (v. 5)?

6. Under pressure, how does the faithful Christian (vv. 5-6) contrast with the person described in verses 6-8?

7. In the context of trials and perseverance, why does James contrast rich and poor Christians (vv. 9-11)?

8. In what ways do you tend to rely on your possessions?

9. How are temptations different from trials (vv. 2-16)?

10. What role does God play when we face trials and when we face temptations (vv. 2-16)?

11. How is God the ultimate example of goodness and dependability (vv. 16-18)?

How is this a source of joy and hope for you?

12. Think of trials or temptations you are currently facing. How can this passage encourage you to depend on God?

13. Take time now to talk to God about your needs. Ask him to help you be like him in his goodness and dependability.

3
Words, Words, Words

James 1:19-27

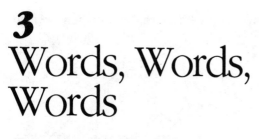

We all do it. It's as common as flies around a horse. While someone else is talking, we're thinking about what we're going to say next instead of about what is being said to us. We know others are worth more care and attention. But the habit is hard to break.

God wants us to slow down and listen too. But even when we've really listened to him, we're still not done. This study gives us practical help on listening and more.

1. How do you feel when someone really hears you?

Why is it so difficult to be a good listener?

2. Read James 1:19-27. How can being quick to listen and slow to speak help us be slow to become angry (v. 19)?

3. How could the commands in verse 19 affect the way your small group or Christian fellowship interacts?

4. When have you experienced the truth that "man's anger does not bring about the righteous life that God desires" (v. 20)?

5. James tells us that God's Word was planted in us. What weeds can choke that Word and keep it from growing (v. 21)? Explain.

6. In your own words explain how the person who merely listens is different from the one who puts God's Word into practice (vv. 22-25).

7. Why is there a tendency for Christians to listen to and yet not to follow God's Word?

How can you avoid this tendency?

8. According to verses 26 and 27 how do people who *think* they are religious differ from those who are truly religious?

9. How do these verses summarize what God desires from us?

10. Give some specific examples of how your religion could become more "pure and faultless"?

11. Based on what you've read in this chapter, do you think James would be satisfied with good works apart from our listening to and receiving God's Word? Explain.

12. Ask God to help you become a better listener and doer of his Word.

4
Who's the Judge?
James 2:1-13

Labels are found more places than on soup cans. We put them on people all the time. Funny or dull. Educated or uneducated. Friendly or cold. There are all kinds of ways we can categorize people. And our categories can have a profound influence on the way we treat people. As you might suspect, James has a few words to say about favoritism.

1. What kinds of things make you favor one person more than another?

2. Read James 2:1-13. Why should believing in "our glorious Lord Jesus Christ" (v. 1) keep us from showing favoritism?

3. How would you react if someone came into your church who wore sloppy clothes, was dirty or had body odor (vv. 2-4)?

4. Why do many people give preferential treatment to those who have money?

Why is it wrong to make distinctions in this way (v. 4)?

5. Verse 5 says God has chosen the poor to be rich in faith. Is God guilty of showing favoritism in this way? Explain.

Why is it easier to have faith when you are poor than when you are rich?

6. From a practical standpoint, why was it foolish for early Christians to favor the rich over the poor (vv. 6-7)?

To what extent is James's description of the rich valid today?

7. How can "the royal law" (v. 8) guide our treatment of both poor and rich?

8. How do verses 9-11 emphasize the seriousness of treating people unequally?

9. In what sense is violating one law as serious as breaking every law?

10. How will the way we speak and act toward others affect the way God treats us (vv. 12-13)?

11. How can the cross, the ultimate example of mercy triumphing over judgment, be a model for the way we interact with others?

12. Think of ways in which you show favoritism. Ask God to help you change your attitudes and actions.

5
Just
Works

James 2:14-26

It is easier said than done" is a cliché that certainly applies to our Christian life. It is much easier to talk about God than to obey him. James said, "Even the demons believe there is one God." But that certainly does not make them Christians! That's why someone can have all his doctrine perfectly straight and still have missed out on God's will. James helps us stay on target.

---

1. What are some ways we don't put actions behind our words?

---

2. Read James 2:14-26. According to James, what good is faith without deeds (vv. 14-17)? Explain why.

---

3. What objection does James anticipate (v. 18)?

How does he answer it (vv. 18-19)?

_____

4. Why is mere intellectual agreement to truth not enough (v. 19)?

_____

5. James gives two Old Testament examples of faith in action. The first is the familiar story of God testing Abraham by asking him to sacrifice his son Isaac. Abraham obeyed but was stopped by an angel at the last minute (see Gen 22). How was Abraham's faith made complete by what he did (2:21-24)?

_____

6. The second example is Rahab, the prostitute who hid two Israelite spies sent to Jericho before Israel's attack (see Josh 2). How did Rahab's belief affect her (Jas 2:25)?

_____

7. How do your actions demonstrate the reality of your faith?

8. How does James's closing analogy (v. 26) summarize his teaching on faith and actions?

9. Does James ever say that works without faith can save? What does this imply about faith?

10. In what ways can you bring your actions more in line with your beliefs?

11. Talk to God about ways he can lead you into a more consistent Christian life.

6
On Preventing Forest Fires

James 3:1-12

Oe of the most distressing crises is a fire out of control. The pain of seeing the resulting destruction can be almost unbearable. Personal belongings going up in smoke. The beauty of nature destroyed. Even loss of life itself. In this passage James compares the destructive power of the tongue to that of a forest fire.

---

1. How do you respond to the adage, "Sticks and stones may break my bones, but words will never hurt me"?

---

2. Read James 3:1-12. James suggests that not many people should become teachers (v. 1). What examples come to your mind of religious teachers whose lives people judged more strictly than others?

Why were they judged more harshly?

3. Why do you think people often give advice they don't follow themselves?

4. James compares the tongue to a bit and a rudder (vv. 3-4). Why do you think the tongue has such control over our lives?

5. James also compares the tongue to a fire and to a world of evil (vv. 5-6). What is the point of these two comparisons?

6. Verses 7-8 emphasize what a challenge it is to control the tongue. What makes this so difficult?

7. In what ways can the tongue poison people and relationships?

8. In verses 9-12 James uses a series of analogies from nature (springs, trees, vines). How do they highlight the inconsistencies of the tongue?

9. James has focused primarily on the destructive power of the tongue. In what ways can the tongue also bring refreshment and healing?

---

10. What can you do to give God more praise? Be specific.

How can you give more praise to those you come in contact with each day?

---

11. Ask God to make your tongue a source of life rather than a source of destruction.

7
Makers and Breakers of Peace
James 3:13—4:10

Why do people who love each other the most often fight the most too? Husbands and wives, parents and children, brothers and sisters—it's all too common. James offers a valuable remedy for this sickness.

1. Does your family ever quarrel? Why do these fights and arguments erupt?

2. Read James 3:13—4:10. In 3:13-18 James discusses earthly and heavenly wisdom. What are the characteristics of each?

3. How might earthly wisdom provoke fights and quarrels?

4. How might wisdom from heaven help us resolve conflicts we face?

5. What does James say is the source of quarrels (4:1-2)?

6. In Buddhist philosophy, desire is said to be the source of all suffering. To combat suffering we should simply stop desiring. In contrast, how does James say we should deal with our desires (vv. 2-3)?

7. Why do we often fail to ask God for what we want?

8. James says we don't receive even when we ask because we ask with wrong motives (v. 3). What might be some examples of right and wrong motives in prayer?

9. What else does James say is necessary in order to come to God in prayer (vv. 4-10)?

10. What does it mean to be humble, to submit to God (vv. 6-7)?

11. In verses 7-10 James gives several suggestions for humbling ourselves before God. How does each contribute to a humble spirit?

12. Are there situations where humility could help you become a source of peace this coming week? Explain.

13. Take a few minutes to quietly humble yourself before God. Ask him to help you become a peacemaker during the next several days.

8
Getting Perspective
James 4:11-17

I am the master of my fate. I am the captain of my soul." How subtly we convince ourselves that we control our lives. Sometimes only a crisis or even death itself convinces us otherwise. If we are truly wise and humble, we will listen carefully when James says, "You are a mist that appears for a little while and then vanishes."

1. If you knew you were going to die tomorrow, how would your attitude toward life today be different?

2. Read James 4:11-17. Why does James say we shouldn't slander or speak against a Christian brother or sister (vv. 11-12)?

3. How do we tend to build ourselves up by criticizing others?

4. If we judge the law, what does this say about our attitude toward the lawgiver?

5. How can a proper attitude toward God (v. 12) enable us to have a proper attitude toward others?

6. How would you describe the two attitudes toward the future found in verses 13-17?

7. James compares life to a mist (v. 14). How does a sudden death, especially that of a famous person, help us to realize this?

8. How do you feel about your life being like a mist?

9. If our life is like a mist, what should be our attitude toward tomorrow?

Is James saying it is wrong to plan for the future? Explain.

---

10. How does our attitude toward the future relate to what James has said previously about humility?

---

11. In verse 17 James says it is a sin not to do good when we know we should. How is this sin like boasting?

---

12. Ask God to help you love those around you rather than judge them. Humbly commit your future plans to the Lord.

9
What Awaits

James 5:1-11

You have probably heard of the young man who cried out, "Lord, I want patience and I want it now!" James encourages us in this passage to wait on God, to be patient, and warns us against wanting it all now.

1. How does our society encourage impatience?

2. Read James 5:1-11. Into what two sections is this passage divided, and who is addressed in each?

3. James declares that misery awaits rich people. What crimes have they committed (vv. 1-6)?

4. How will their wealth testify against them in the last judgment?

Is James condemning all rich people? Explain.

5. How is piling up riches the opposite of patience that waits in faith for God to provide?

6. When are you tempted to hoard rather than to give and wait on God?

7. Why do you think James begins the second section in verse 7 with, "Be patient"?

8. James goes on to give three examples of patient people: a farmer, the prophets and Job. How is each an example of patience?

9. In what areas of your life are you impatient?

In what ways could you learn patience from the three examples James mentions?

10. The Lord's coming provides a backdrop for James's word to the rich and to those who suffer. What different reactions would you expect each group to have to the prospect of the Lord's return (vv. 7-9)?

11. How can Christ's return affect such practical matters as our use of wealth and emotional matters as our response to suffering?

12. Thank God for the practical help James gives in becoming more patient. Ask God to help you apply his message to the areas in your life that need patience.

10
Making Others Whole

James 5:12-20

Broken homes, shattered relationships, damaged emotions—we live in a fragmented and hurting society. As we see all the wounded people around us, we long to help, to offer a healing touch. James gives us very practical suggestions for helping people to become whole.

1. Why do you think our society is so fragmented?

2. Read James 5:12-20. How does verse 12 reinforce the themes the tongue (3:1-12) and of patience (4:9-11)?

3. Do you pray more when you are in trouble or when things are going well?

What balance does James suggest in verse 13?

4. In verses 14-16 James discusses physical and spiritual healing. What are the steps in this process?

5. How is physical healing connected with forgiveness of sins?

6. Would you call elders for anointing, prayer and confession? Why or why not?

7. How can we provide other opportunities for mutual confession and prayer (v. 16)?

8. How does Elijah illustrate the effectiveness of prayer (vv. 17-18)?

9. What different types of prayer are mentioned in verses 13-18?

---

10. What steps could you take to make one of these types of prayer more a part of your life?

---

11. According to verses 19-20, how, if at all, are we our brother's keeper?

---

12. Summarize what verses 13-20 teach us about how we can help people to become whole physically, emotionally or spiritually.

---

13. Ask God for grace in this ministry.

11
Faith That Works: James Review
James 1—5

Y ou have endured. You have persevered. You have been dependable. You have made it through James! May your faith be stronger as
a result of your time in this letter.

---

1. What changes have you seen in yourself since you began this study?

---

2. Quickly reread James 1—5. What major topics were discussed in
this letter?

How do these topics help us understand James's view of Christian
maturity?

3. What unifying theme, if any, did you see in James?

4. Why is perseverance so important for Christians (see especially 1:1-18)?

5. How is James's view of religion (1:26-27) developed in other chapters?

6. Some people claim that James is an antifaith letter. How would you respond to that claim?

7. What examples does James give of faith and actions working together?

8. How does 5:7-20 act as a summary of the letter?

9. From your study of James, what one area of your Christian life is in most need of endurance and consistency?

10. What steps are you taking (will you take) to work on that?

11. How have you been encouraged by studying this letter?

12. Thank God for what you have learned from studying the book of James.

Leader's Notes

Leading a Bible discussion can be an enjoyable and rewarding experience. But it can also be *scary*—especially if you've never done it before. If this is your feeling, you're in good company. When God asked Moses to lead the Israelites out of Egypt, he replied, "O Lord, please send someone else to do it!" (Ex 4:13).

When Solomon became king of Israel, he felt the task was far beyond his abilities. "I am only a little child and do not know how to carry out my duties. . . . Who is able to govern this great people of yours?" (1 Kings 3:7, 9).

When God called Jeremiah to be a prophet, he replied, "Ah, Sovereign LORD, . . . I do not know how to speak; I am only a child" (Jer 1:6).

The list goes on. The apostles were "unschooled, ordinary men" (Acts 4:13). Timothy was young, frail and frightened. Paul's "thorn in the flesh" made him feel weak. But God's response to all of his servants—including you—is essentially the same: "My grace is sufficient for you" (2 Cor 12:9). Relax. God helped these people in spite of their weaknesses, and he can help you in spite of your feelings of inadequacy.

There is another reason why you should feel encouraged. Leading a Bible discussion is not difficult if you follow certain guidelines. You don't need to be an expert on the Bible or a trained teacher. The suggestions listed below should enable you to effectively and enjoyably fulfill your role as leader.

Preparing to Lead

1. Ask God to help you understand and apply the passage to your own life. Unless this happens, you will not be prepared to lead others. Pray too for the various members of the group. Ask God to give you an enjoyable and profitable time together studying his Word.

2. As you begin each study, read and reread the assigned Bible passage to familiarize yourself with what the author is saying. In the case of book studies, you may want to read through the entire book prior to the first study. This will give you a helpful overview of its contents.

3. This study guide is based on the New International Version of the Bible. It will help you and the group if you use this translation as the basis for your study and discussion. Encourage others to use the NIV also, but allow them the freedom to use whatever translation they prefer.

4. Carefully work through each question in the study. Spend time in meditation and reflection as you formulate your answers.

5. Write your answers in the space provided in the study guide. This will help you to express your understanding of the passage clearly.

6. It might help you to have a Bible dictionary handy. Use it to look up any unfamiliar words, names or places. (For additional help on how to study a passage, see chapter five of *Leading Bible Discussions,* IVP.)

7. Once you have finished your own study of the passage, familiarize yourself with the leader's notes for the study you are leading. These are designed to help you in several ways. First, they tell you the purpose the study guide author had in mind while writing the study. Take time to think through how the study questions work together to accomplish that purpose. Second, the notes provide you with additional background information or comments on some of the questions. This information can be useful if people have difficulty understanding or answering a question. Third, the leader's notes can alert you to potential problems you may encounter during the study.

8. If you wish to remind yourself of anything mentioned in the leader's notes, make a note to yourself below that question in the study.

Leading the Study

1. Begin the study on time. Unless you are leading an evangelistic Bible study, open with prayer, asking God to help you to understand and apply the passage.

2. Be sure that everyone in your group has a study guide. Encourage them to prepare beforehand for each discussion by working through the questions in the guide.

3. At the beginning of your first time together, explain that these studies are meant to be discussions not lectures. Encourage the members of the group to participate. However, do not put pressure on those who may be hesitant to speak during the first few sessions.

4. Read the introductory paragraph at the beginning of the discussion. This will orient the group to the passage being studied.

5. Read the passage aloud if you are studying one chapter or less. You may choose to do this yourself, or someone else may read if he or she has been asked to do so prior to the study. Longer passages may occasionally be read in parts at different times during the study. Some studies may cover several chapters. In such cases reading aloud would probably take too much time, so the group members should simply read the assigned passages prior to the study.

6. As you begin to ask the questions in the guide, keep several things in mind. First, the questions are designed to be used just as they are written. If you wish, you may simply read them aloud to the group. Or you may prefer to express them in your own words. However, unnecessary rewording of the questions is not recommended.

Second, the questions are intended to guide the group toward understanding and applying the *main idea* of the passage. The author of the guide has stated his or her view of this central idea in the *purpose* of the study in the leader's notes. You should try to understand how the passage expresses this idea and how the study questions work together to lead the group in that direction.

There may be times when it is appropriate to deviate from the study guide. For example, a question may have already been answered. If so, move on to the next question. Or someone may raise an important question not covered in the guide. Take time to discuss it! The important thing is to use discretion. There may be many routes you can travel to reach the goal of the study. But the easiest route is usually the one the author has suggested.

7. Avoid answering your own questions. If necessary, repeat or rephrase them until they are clearly understood. An eager group quickly becomes passive and silent if they think the leader will do most of the talking.

8. Don't be afraid of silence. People may need time to think about the question before formulating their answers.

9. Don't be content with just one answer. Ask, "What do the rest of you think?" or "Anything else?" until several people have given answers to the question.

10. Acknowledge all contributions. Try to be affirming whenever possible. Never reject an answer. If it is clearly wrong, ask, "Which verse led you to that conclusion?" or again, "What do the rest of you think?"

11. Don't expect every answer to be addressed to you, even though this will probably happen at first. As group members become more at ease, they will begin to truly interact with each other. This is one sign of a healthy discussion.

12. Don't be afraid of controversy. It can be very stimulating. If you don't resolve an issue completely, don't be frustrated. Move on and keep it in mind for later. A subsequent study may solve the problem.

13. Stick to the passage under consideration. It should be the source for answering the questions. Discourage the group from unnecessary cross-referencing. Likewise, stick to the subject and avoid going off on tangents.

14. Periodically summarize what the *group* has said about the passage. This helps to draw together the various ideas mentioned and gives continuity to the study. But don't preach.

15. Conclude your time together with conversational prayer. Be sure to ask God's help to apply those things which you learned in the study.

16. End on time.

Many more suggestions and helps are found in *Leading Bible Discussions* (IVP). Reading and studying through that would be well worth your time.

Components of Small Groups

A healthy small group should do more than study the Bible. There are four components you should consider as you structure your time together.

Nurture. Being a part of a small group should be a nurturing and edifying experience. You should grow in your knowledge and love of God and each other. If we are to properly love God, we must know and keep his commandments (Jn 14:15). That is why Bible study should be a foundational part of your small group. But you can be nurtured by other things as well. You can memorize Scripture, read and discuss a book, or occasionally listen to a tape of a good speaker.

Community. Most people have a need for close friendships. Your small group can be an excellent place to cultivate such relationships. Allow time for informal interaction before and after the study. Have a time of sharing during the meeting. Do fun things together as a group, such as a potluck supper or a picnic. Have someone bring refreshments to the meeting. Be creative!

Worship. A portion of your time together can be spent in worship and prayer. Praise God together for who he is. Thank him for what he has done and is doing in your lives and in the world. Pray for each other's needs. Ask God to help you to apply what you have learned. Sing hymns together.

Mission. Many small groups decide to work together in some form of outreach. This can be a practical way of applying what you have learned. You can host a series of evangelistic discussions for your friends or neighbors. You can visit people at a home for the elderly. Help a widow with cleaning or repair jobs around her home. Such projects can have a transforming influence on your group.

For a detailed discussion of the nature and function of small groups, read *Small Group Leaders' Handbook* or *Good Things Come in Small Groups* (both from IVP).

Study 1. Faith That Works: James Overview. James 1—5.

Purpose: To gain an overview of the main points of James.

As the leader, you need to work through the study before consulting the leader's notes. You have to deal with the passage personally to lead the group as effectively as possible. So if you have not yet done study 1, do so now. Then come back here.

Finished? Great. Let's hit some practical matters first. Begin the study by taking five minutes to explain that the group will be learning by discussion, by each person's contribution, which will be stimulated by a few thought-provoking questions. Review the "Suggestions for Group Study" (p. 7).

Summarize the key points from the introduction about the person James and the people to whom he wrote his letter. Be sure to mention that he did not follow Jesus until after the resurrection, that he became the head of the early church in Jerusalem, that he was very aware of the potential for conflicts between Jewish-Christians and Gentile-Christians, and that he died a martyr's death. Regarding the recipients of the letter, note that it is not certain if James was writing exclusively to Jewish-Christians or to all Christians outside Palestine. In any case, the letter was not addressed to a specific congregation (as most of Paul's letters were).

This summary will help group members to answer questions 2 and 3. Even if each member has a copy of this guide and has read the introduction, you should talk briefly about James and his audience.

Question 1. Every study begins with an "approach" question, which is meant to be asked before the passage is read. These questions are important for several reasons.

First, they help the group to warm up to each other. No matter how well a group may know each other, there is always a stiffness that needs to be overcome before people will begin to talk openly. A good question will break the ice.

Second, approach questions get people thinking along the lines of the topic of the study. Most people will have lots of different things going on in their minds (dinner, an important meeting coming up, how to get the car fixed) that will have nothing to do with the study. A creative question will get their attention and draw them into the discussion.

Third, approach questions can reveal where our thoughts or feelings need to be transformed by Scripture. This is why it is especially important not to read the passage before the approach question is asked. The passage will tend to color the honest reactions people would otherwise give because they are of course supposed to think the way the Bible does. Giving honest responses to various issues before they find out what the Bible says may help them to see where their thoughts or attitudes need to be changed.

Question 2. There are three ways to handle the reading of the letter. First, you could read the entire letter aloud. This could be done by one person, but we recommend that several people take, for example, one chapter each. This will help avoid the possible monotony or fatigue of one person reading the whole book. It will take about fifteen minutes to do this. Second, everyone could read the letter silently. You need to allow ten minutes for this. Third, if you are sure everyone in the group has read the letter already, you could take five minutes for each person to scan it. Be sure to use the first or second option if someone has not read it. Otherwise that person will be lost during the study.

Again, note that background information is needed to answer this question. As James was the head of the church in Jerusalem, he had reason to be authoritative. He didn't live in a hole, however. He was quite aware of human nature and had often dealt with people's problems. Be sure to note how he describes himself in 1:1. What does this say about James?

Question 3. One thing we learn about those to whom James wrote is that they were mostly poor or middle class (2:5-7; 5:7-8), though not exclusively so (1:9-11; 5:1-6). They were also people just like us, with problems as well as potential for change.

Question 9. This question will help you know what problems to expect in the following studies. Someone will likely mention the faith-works issue raised in James 2. Another person might feel James is too harsh on the rich. Don't try to answer the difficulties that people bring up. Simply allow them to express themselves. But at the end of the study, be sure to say that you will grapple with those questions in the coming studies—and be sure you do!

Study 2. Dependable or Double-minded? James 1:1-18.

Purpose: To understand the importance perseverance when we face trials and temptations.

This is a key study in this series. Perseverance is a theme which permeates the entire book, though not always explicitly. As James goes on to deal with judging others, the tongue, possessions and other topics, the theme of perseverance is not far in the background.

Question 3. Confusion could arise about what perseverance is all about. You may want to make sure your group's understanding of perseverance is adequate. James is not talking about stubbornness or grinning and bearing it.

Question 6. This may elicit questions about the place of doubt in the Christian life. While periods of questioning can be healthy and allow for growth, a life characterized by indecisiveness is worthless in God's sight. James draws two extremes to make his point.

Question 7. James's second contrast (vv. 9-11) also shows the value of perseverance. When the rich hit a crisis, they turn to God, and this is good. When the poor have something good happen, they seldom give themselves the credit (as the rich might be inclined to do). The poor know it had to come from God, and so they turn to him in thanks. Each situation increases reliance on God.

Thus depending on the makeup of your group, you may want to change question 7 to, "How has good fortune turned you toward God?"

Question 11. The first fruits of the harvest were specifically committed to God as part of the regular thanksgiving of each Israelite (see Lev

23:9-11). The term is often used as a metaphor to signify priority of position and importance in God's sight (for example, Jer 2:3 RSV).

Study 3. Words, Words, Words. James 1:19-27.

Purpose: To learn to listen to others and to the Word, and to put the Word into practice.

James begins his elaboration of the theme of leading a consistent Christian life by focusing on the place of words in our lives. Your goal as leader is to bring out how we should handle words as Christians and how we should go beyond words to actions.

Question 1. There's more than one answer to each of these approach questions. Allow the responses to come from the broad experiences each person brings to the group. The answers to these questions are not intended to be drawn from the passage but from our knowledge of human nature in general.

Question 2. Is anger always a sin? Doesn't Paul say, "Be angry but do not sin" (Eph 4:26 RSV)? Isn't there an appropriate time for anger? When we hear about child abuse, isn't anger justified? These are some questions you could hear from the group members in response to verses 19-20. We are not justified in becoming angry in defense of ourselves. We may, however, find ourselves within the bounds of God's righteous anger when genuine evil and injustice are involved. Even so, God is "compassionate and gracious, slow to anger, abounding in love" (Ps 103:8). We ought to be as well.

Question 3. This question can offer an opportunity for reflection on how people are interacting in the Bible study itself. Are they acting Christianly among themselves? Do some dominate discussion? Do others constantly change the subject or take the group to other parts of Scripture? Does anyone follow up with questions when someone begins to open up with problems or deep concerns? If not, how can the group grow in these areas?

Question 6. "The perfect law" mentioned in James 1:25 is the new covenant. Christ completed the old covenant, setting us free to be in harmony with God and with ourselves (see Jer 31:31-34 and Mt 5:17).

Question 8. Some are likely to object to James's description of pure and genuine religion in verse 27. Note, however, that he does not say this is all that true religion is. Nevertheless, it does cover things pretty well. The phrase *orphans and widows* is a general reference to all in need of help, while *to keep oneself from being polluted by the world* encourages us to adopt godly values, attitudes and virtues.

Study 4. Who's the Judge? James 2:1-13.

Purpose: To learn to treat others as God treats us.

Question 1. Some possible answers (if people are honest) might include: "If they have personalities I can get along with." "How much they accept me." "What they have accomplished in life." "How they look." As with all approach questions, accept all answers without comment—except to help people clarify or expand on their answers. Wait till later in the study to apply James's teaching to these initial responses.

Question 3. Even if your church or fellowship group has a large number of poor folk in it, some people have very strong ideas about what is appropriate Sunday attire. Otherwise you may want to skip this question.

Question 5. Is God guilty of favoritism? Perhaps he is just trying to even the odds, so to speak, compensating the poor spiritually for what they might lack materially.

If God has chosen the poor (see Ps 140:12; Prov 19:17; Lk 1:52-53; 6:20-25), does this mean the rich (and most people in North America are rich compared to the rest of the world) are automatically rejected by God? If such a question is raised, direct the group back to James for the answer. You might also direct them to 1:9-11 where James points out how God helps both poor and rich to trust in him.

Some might also suggest that James is speaking of the poor in spirit in verse 5. Yet the context of 2:1-4 and the way the poor are dishonored as described in 2:6-7 indicate he means the materially poor.

Question 8. Verses 10-11 might also raise some objections. Try not to get sidetracked on whether stealing a pencil is as bad as murder. Others might also say, "Well, if I'm condemned for a lie, I might as well commit adultery." James's point is that in the eyes of the law, a transgression is a transgression. This emphasizes the seriousness of acting in a prejudiced manner.

Question 9. This question gets to the heart of the issue raised in the first question. Even a "minor" sin is serious, not just because a rule is violated, but because the special relationship God intends to have with human beings is broken.

Questions 10-11. While James says very little directly about Christ in his letter, it is shot through with Christ's teaching and with a theology that is rooted in the center of the Christian faith. In this case, mercy triumphs over judgment for each sinner who, condemned to eternal punishment (judgment), is granted forgiveness (mercy) by accepting the substitution of Christ's death for his own. Thus we should act as those who have been set free and not hold tightly to our judgment of (unwillingness to forgive) others. This, of course, is the very teaching we find in the Lord's Prayer (forgive as we forgive others—Mt 6:12) and in Christ's parable of the unmerciful steward (Mt 18:21-35).

Study 5. Just Works. James 2:14-26.

Purpose: To see how what we believe needs to be matched by the way we live.

This could well be your most controversial discussion in James. This passage has certainly raised more questions about the book of James than anything else. It was primarily because of the seeming emphasis on salvation by works that Martin Luther virtually booted this epistle out of his Bible. Many people mistakenly assume that James is in a direct debate with Paul and that the two are taking opposing positions. Yet such is not the case. James's emphasis is that true faith is evidenced by works, not that works alone is sufficient or that works and faith in combination save. Verses 18 and 22 make this point as well. When in verse 24 James says, "not by faith alone," he is speaking of the kind of faith the demons possess—mere intellectual assent, which cannot save. Such a position does not contradict Paul at all, who made a similar point. Compare James 2:14 with Titus 1:16 and Ephesians 2:8-10.

Many Christians are doctrinally orthodox but fail to be orthodox in the outworking of their faith. Their faith is all in their head and not in their actions. This is the sort of person James seeks to touch. And this should be the emphasis you give to the study as well. While the whole book helps us put our faith into practice, this passage specifically aims to controvert the fallacy that right doctrine and "nice" words are sufficient. Real faith is always indicated by works. If there are no works, the faith is not real. It cannot save. Rather, the kind of faith that can and does save always results in Christian action. This was the case with Abraham as well as with Rahab.

Question 3. One way of paraphrasing the first part of verse 18 is, "Different people have different gifts. Some might have the gift of faith. Others might have the gift of good works. James, you put too much emphasis on the combination of the two."

Question 4. Many people know the doctrines of Christianity and may even believe them to be true. But they may have never made a commitment to Jesus Christ, placing their trust in him as their Savior and Lord.

Question 7. Many groups will be concerned about whether or not James contradicts Paul on the issue of faith and works. If you anticipate that your group will want to discuss this, you may want to add the following question between questions 7 and 8: "James says, 'A person is justified by what he does and not by faith alone' (v. 24). How can this be reconciled with Paul's teaching that we are justified by faith and not by works (Rom 4:4-5; Eph 2:8-9)?" Note that, in addition to the different way Paul and James may be using the word *faith*, they may also be using the word *justification* in different ways. For Paul it means to be declared righteous. For James it may mean to prove the validity of faith.

Question 9. This question can be crucial if some in the group believe James is advocating salvation by works alone. Don't miss it.

Question 10. Give people time to reflect and to share if they desire. If those present have a hard time thinking of any discrepancies between their beliefs and their actions, maybe the group should discuss how each can observe his or her own actions more critically.

Study 6. On Preventing Forest Fires. James 3:1-12.

Purpose: To learn how our words can bring healing rather than harm.

James has structured this passage to explain the substantial respon-sibilities and risks taken by teachers. James does this through a series of analogies which explain the power of the tongue (vv. 3-4), the difficulty in controlling the tongue (vv. 5-8), and the gross inconsis-tencies possible with the tongue (vv. 9-12). The questions themselves are thus structured around these explanations. Obviously James's words apply far beyond teachers. We can all find ourselves in this passage. Your task is to help the group members do just this.

Question 1. Ask whether people agree or disagree and why. Ask if they have found it to be true in their own lives. Have words ever hurt them?

Question 2. Not only do teachers have responsibilities to teach what is right and true and what is not, they also will be judged by the standards they themselves tell others to live up to. That is why it is so scandalous when we hear of religious leaders who have fallen victim to greed or lust or lying. We expect more from them (as does the world) because they are the ones who are upholding God's high standards of truth and love. Politicians or entertainers who engage in the same sinful conduct are not judged nearly so harshly by the public.

At the same time, James makes the point throughout this passage that the tongue is a powerful instrument, immensely difficult to con-trol, though very potent when it is controlled (like a rudder on a ship or a bit in a horse's mouth). Since words are the chief tool of a teacher, he is more responsible than most to use words correctly and help-fully.

Question 7. You may be able to skip this question if the topic of destructive criticism has been adequately covered in question 1.

Question 10. This is an important question. Proper use of the tongue is not just controlling the negative but funneling the positive to pos-itive use—just as a tamed horse can be put to constructive purposes.

Look up *praise* in a Bible dictionary if you can't define it adequately yourself. Most people would be hard pressed to praise God in prayer for five minutes. Why? Most people would be hard pressed to praise even a close friend for five minutes. Why? How can these be overcome? You can only help your group grapple honestly with these issues through follow-up questions if you have dealt with them in your own life. Go back and see if you are satisfied with your own answers.

Study 7. Makers and Breakers of Peace. James 3:13—4:10.
Purpose: To understand the sources of quarrels and the sources of peace.

Everyone gets into arguments, some more frequently than others. James is seeking to identify the sources of quarrels and how they can be avoided. The sources are envy and self-ambition. The solution is humility before God and others. Keep these two things in mind as you lead.

Studies 7 and 8 could quite easily be entitled "Humility I" and "Humility II." The passage is split simply because it would be too long to discuss adequately in one hour. Study 7 approaches humility from the perspective of making and breaking peace. To be a peacemaker you need humility. Study 8 approaches humility more directly. How do you view yourself in relation to God, others and the future? Do you put others down to build yourself up? Do you feel competent to do good on your own?

You might think of this study as being in two halves—3:13-18 and 4:1-10. Humility is the implied solution to quarrels in the first half (accepting God's wisdom rather than your own). It is made explicit, however, in the second half.

Question 9. The difficulty in translating verse 5 is evidenced by the fact that the NIV offers three possibilities, none of which makes very much sense. Likely the verse means either that God's indwelling Spirit and sinful envy are not compatible in God's people (a thought very similar to that of verse 4) or that God is a jealous husband (Ex 20:5; 34:14; Deut 4:24) who will not tolerate divided loyalty by his bride.

Study 8. Getting Perspective. James 4:11-17.
Purpose: To identify my attitude toward God, others and the future, and to learn how to make them what they should be.

Questions 2-4. If there is some question about how we judge the law (v. 11), you could ask, "In what sense are we judging the law when we speak against others?"

To criticize another person is to break the command to love one's neighbor, or to say in effect, "I have decided (judged) that the law really isn't a good one and doesn't apply in this case. For, you see, I am above the law (being the judge of when it applies and when it doesn't) and am free to break it by being critical of another person."

Question 6-8. The point of the mist analogy is not that life is insignificant but that it is temporary. Note that it is set in contrast to verse 13, which expresses the attitude that life will go on indefinitely and that I am in control.

Some group members may have never considered that their life is temporary. In fact, they may even refuse to accept this during the study itself. "Oh, I never think about that." "You can't live like there's no tomorrow." Be ready to bring the discussion back to what James says, asking the group to look to the passage for answers if no conclusions develop.

Study 9. What Awaits. James 5:1-11.
Purpose: To see the importance of patience in our lives.

This passage discusses two seemingly disconnected topics—hoarding (coveting, materialism) and patience. Your concern as group leader is to highlight the ways these two actually intertwine.

Question 2. This is a very important observation question. Do not skip it because it may seem too easy. Make sure the group knows that the second section begins with verse 7.

Question 5. This may throw some people. But don't be put off. Persist in seeking a response. Essentially hoarding means you can't wait to have something or that things control you (have priority in your life). You must possess all you can because you are afraid you might never get what you want or that you might lose it later. You can't wait day by day on God. Patience, by definition, waits. It is an act of faith that God is good, that he will provide. We don't have to anxiously work because we fear he won't come through. We can relax in confidence in him.

Question 7. Here is connection number two between hoarding and patience. Hoarding creates hardships for others. It makes it necessary for them to be patient, to wait for God's justice to prevail.

Question 8. Feel free to take time on this question. Obviously, a farmer can't harvest in the spring. He has to wait until fall. Likewise, if a prophet foretells what will happen in the future, by definition it won't happen now. He has to wait to be proven correct. (Hebrews 11:32-38 could also offer you a quick summary of the patience and triumphs of the prophets.) Job endured great suffering, losing his possessions, his children and his health. He had to wait for God to vindicate him, to show that he was not suffering as punishment for sin.

Question 9. The key to application lies in these questions. For example, it was what Job knew and learned about God that gave him his patience. The same can be true for us. If we know God is completely generous, wise and sovereign, for example, we can trust him to give us all we need at the time best for us. We need not pile up riches impatiently, untrustingly.

Question 10. Many Christians today look forward excitedly to Christ's return, little realizing that the judgments he will deal out may be on them and their nation. Be aware if such misconceptions are common in your group.

Study 10. Making Others Whole. James 5:12-20.

Purpose: To grow in prayer and in helping others.

Don't be deceived. This is not a short study. Even though it covers only nine verses, you will need to gauge your time carefully. Several potentially controversial topics lurk in this passage—faith healing, and the church's role in it, is most notable among them. The place of prayer in one's life also deserves time so the group members can get the concrete help needed in weak areas.

This pastoral section of James deserves a pastoral tone, which you can set. James concerns himself with the needs (physical and spiritual) of those in the body. You should too.

Question 2. Verse 12 can be seen as the beginning of a review of themes covered so far in the letter, such as the tongue, faith, sin and the like. For example, James reinforces the theme of patience in that taking the Lord's name in vain is one of the most frequent manifestations of impatience.

Question 4. It is important to note that the sick person initiates the healing process for several reasons: (1) psychologically people are most likely to receive help if they see their own need; (2) we should be cautious about forcing help on those who do not want it; (3) James makes it clear that this is one permissible way to deal with illness (there is no *must* in the sentence). It is hoped that these points will flow from the questions here as the discussion progresses.

Olive oil was used both internally and externally for medicinal purposes. It was also used in religious ceremonies of consecration (Ex 29:2) and purification (Lev 14:10-18). It symbolized gladness, comfort and spiritual nourishment.

Question 8. See 1 Kings 17:1; 18:1, 42.

Study 11. Faith That Works: James Review. James 1—5.

Purpose: To tie together the main emphases in James.

There are many topics considered by James in this letter. And it has probably been ten weeks since you started moving through the letter. This study offers you a chance to remind yourselves of the various issues raised in the letter and to tie them together so each person comes away with the feeling, "I've got a handle on James now. I know what the book is about."

Question 2. Again, as with study 1, you may have the whole book read aloud (15 minutes), have each member read it silently (10 minutes) or let each one skim it (5 minutes).

Question 6. Be sure answers do not just come from chapter 2. Chapters 1 and 5 also raise the issue of faith directly. And each chapter raises it indirectly.

Question 8. Many of the topics found in the first four chapters are reviewed one last time in 5:7-20.

Andrew T. Le Peau is managing editor of InterVarsity Press and the author of Paths of Leadership. *He and his wife, Phyllis, have written several Bible study guides, including* Ephesians *and* One Plus One Equals One.